D1178577

NUREYEV

NUREYEV

Edited and designed by Howard Brown

Phaidon Press Limited
Regent's Wharf
All Saints Street
London N1 9PA

First published 1993
First paperback edition 1995
© 1993 Phaidon Press Limited

ISBN
0 7148 2966 8 (hardback)
0 7148 3470 X (paperback)

A CIP catalogue record for this book
is available from the British Library

Biographical research: Martha Bremser

Printed in Hong Kong

1   Aged 16 in Ufa, 1954

Unknown photographer

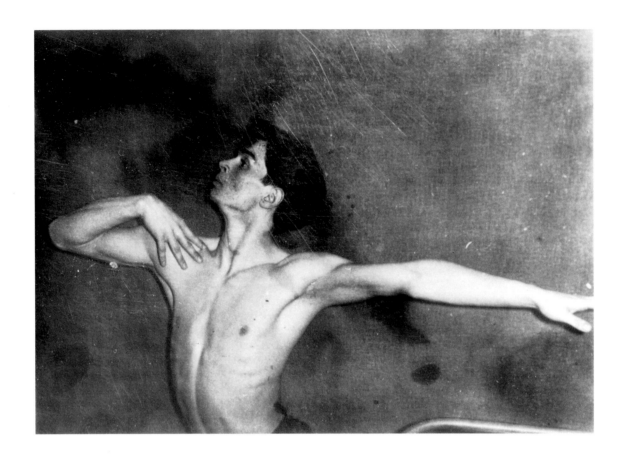

2   Leningrad, 1958

Unknown photographer

3   Leningrad, 1958

Unknown photographer

4   Nureyev with his family (his mother and father in the front row), *c.*1956/7

Unknown photographer

5   Leningrad, *c.*1960

Unknown photographer

6　'Laurencia' with Natalia Dudinskaya, Leningrad, 1960

Unknown photographer

7   'Laurencia' Leningrad, 1961

Unknown photographer

8 'Laurencia' with Nella Tchekova, Leningrad, 1961

Unknown photographer

9 'La Bayadère' Leningrad, 1961

Unknown photographer

10   'The Sleeping Beauty' Kirov Ballet, Paris, May 1961

Agence de Presse Bernand

11/12   Bluebird in 'The Sleeping Beauty' de Cuevas company, Paris, June 1961

Serge Lido

13   With Raymundo de Larrain of the de Cuevas company, Paris, June 1961

14   'The Sleeping Beauty' de Cuevas company, Paris, June 1961

15 'Poème tragique' London, 1961

Reg Wilson

16/17   Portraits, Paris, 1962

Henri Cartier-Bresson

18/19   Rehearsing 'Giselle' with Margot Fonteyn, London, 1962

Reg Wilson

20 Rehearsing 'Giselle' with Margot Fonteyn, London, 1962

Anthony Crickmay

21   Rehearsing 'Giselle' with Margot Fonteyn, London, 1962

Zoë Dominic

22   Rehearsing 'Giselle' with Margot Fonteyn, London, 1962

Houston Rogers

23 Cecil Beaton photographing Nureyev, London, 1962

Zoë Dominic

24/25   'Giselle' with Margot Fonteyn, London, 1962

Mike Davis

26 'Giselle' London, 1962

Houston Rogers

27 'Giselle' with Margot Fonteyn, London, 1962

Zoë Dominic

28   Being photographed for 'Music in Camera' BBC TV, London, 1962

Zoë Dominic

29/30   In rehearsal with Margot Fonteyn (above), London, 1962

Snowdon

31/32   In rehearsal with Margot Fonteyn (above), London, 1962

Snowdon

33/34   In rehearsal with Margot Fonteyn (above), London, 1962

Snowdon

35/36   In rehearsal, London, 1962

Snowdon

38/39 'Le Corsaire' London, 1962

Houston Rogers

40   'Le Corsaire' London, 1962

Houston Rogers

41   In rehearsal, London, 1962

Snowdon

42   'Les Sylphides' London, 1963

Houston Rogers

43/44 'Swan Lake' with Margot Fonteyn, Paris, 1963

46/47 New York, 1963

Elliott Erwitt

49/50   Rehearsing 'Marguerite and Armand' with Margot Fonteyn, London, 1963

Zoë Dominic

51   Rehearsing 'Marguerite and Armand' with Margot Fonteyn, London, 1963

Zoë Dominic

52/53 Rehearsing 'Marguerite and Armand' with Margot Fonteyn, London, 1963

Zoë Dominic

'Marguerite and Armand' London, 1963

Eve Arnold

56 'Marguerite and Armand' with Margot Fonteyn, London, 1963

Anthony Crickmay

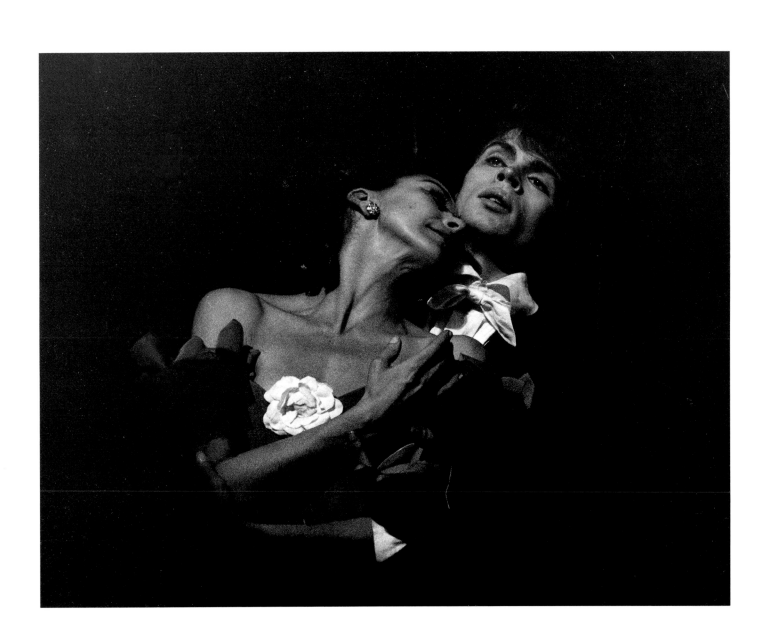

57/58   'Marguerite and Armand' with Margot Fonteyn (left), London, 1963

Cecil Beaton

59/60   'Marguerite and Armand' with Margot Fonteyn (above), London, 1963

Zoë Dominic

61/62 'Marguerite and Armand' with Margot Fonteyn, London, 1963

Zoë Dominic

63/64   'Marguerite and Armand' with Margot Fonteyn, London, 1963

Zoë Dominic

65   'Images of Love' with Lynn Seymour and Christopher Gable, London, 1964

Zoë Dominic

66   Rehearsing 'Gayané' London, 1965

Zoë Dominic

67   Rehearsing 'Raymonda' London, 1964

Zoë Dominic

68   Rehearsing 'Raymonda' with Margot Fonteyn, London, 1964

Jane Bown

69   With Cecil Beaton, 1964

David Bailey

70   'Swan Lake' Vienna, 1964

Snowdon

71   'Romeo and Juliet' with Margot Fonteyn, London, 1965

Zoë Dominic

72　'Prince Igor' London, 1965

Reg Wilson

73/74   Rehearsing with Carla Fracci (above), Milan, 1966

Unknown photographer

75   Rehearsing with Margot Fonteyn, Rome, 1966

76   Milan, 1966

Unknown photographer

78   'Paradise Lost' with Margot Fonteyn, London, 1967

Houston Rogers

79   'Paradise Lost' with Margot Fonteyn, London, 1967

80　'Paradise Lost' with Margot Fonteyn, London, 1967

81 'Paradise Lost' with Margot Fonteyn, London, 1967

Houston Rogers

82   'Paradise Lost' with Margot Fonteyn, London, 1967

Reg Wilson

83   'Paradise Lost' London, 1967

Anthony Crickmay

84/85/86　'Paradise Lost' London, 1967

Zoë Dominic

87/88 'Paradise Lost' London, 1967

Anthony Crickmay

89   Arrest in San Francisco after hippy party, July 1967

(FX5)SAN FRANCISCO,JULY 11(AP)-Rudolph Nureyev, star of the
Royal Ballet, is surrounded by newsmen Tuesday as he sat
on a bench at city prison after release on bail.He and
Margot Fonteyn were arrested by police at a noisy hippie-
land party along with 15 other persons. He answered no ques-
tions. (AP WIREPHOTO) 1967

90/91/92   'Paradise Lost' London, 1967

Zoë Dominic

93   Filming 'Le Jeune Homme et la mort' for TV, Paris, 1967/8

Araldo di Crollalanza

94   'La Bayadère' London, 1968/9

Leslie E. Spatt

95   'Le Corsaire' London, 1968/9

Leslie E. Spatt

96   'Le Corsaire' London, 1969

Zoë Dominic

97　'Pelléas and Mélisande' London, 1969

Houston Rogers

98   'Pelléas and Mélisande' with Margot Fonteyn and Keith Rosson, London, 1969

Anthony Crickmay

99   'The Ropes of Time' London, 1970

Leslie E. Spatt

100   'The Ropes of Time' London, 1970

Zoë Dominic

101   'The Ropes of Time' with Monica Mason, London, 1970

102   'Dances at a Gathering' London, 1970

Unknown photographer

103 'Dances at a Gathering' with Anthony Dowell and David Wall, London, 1970

Leslie E. Spatt

Zoë Dominic

105   'Apollo' Munich, 1970

Unknown photographer

106   'Le Sacre du printemps' Brussels, 1971

Unknown photographer

107   'The Sleeping Beauty' Paris, 1971

Colette Masson

108   'Field Figures' London, 1971

Leslie E. Spatt

109   'Apollo' Paris, 1972

Colette Masson

110/111   'Petrushka' Paris, 1972

Colette Masson

112/113/114   'Apollo' London, 1972/3

115   'Apollo' Paris, 1972

Colette Masson

116   'Agon' London, 1973

Leslie E. Spatt

117   Rehearsing 'The Moor's Pavane' Copenhagen, 1973

118 'Prodigal Son' London, 1973

Leslie E. Spatt

119/120   'Swan Lake' with Natalia Makarova (above), Paris, 1973

Colette Masson

121/122   'Tristan' with Carolyn Carlson, Paris, 1974

Colette Masson

123   'La Fille mal gardée' New York, 1974

MIRA

124   'Apollo' New York, 1974

MIRA

125   'Flower Festival at Genzano' Paris, 1974

Colette Masson

126   'The Sleeping Beauty' with Noella Pontois, Paris, 1974

127   Curtain call after 'Romeo and Juliet' New York, 1974

Linda Vartoogian

128   'La Ventana' with Cynthia Gregory and Erik Bruhn, New York, 1975

129   'Aureole' New York, 1975

Linda Vartoogian

130 'Le Corsaire' with Gelsey Kirkland, New York, 1975

Jack Vartoogian

131　'Night Journey' New York, 1975

Linda Vartoogian

132　　Three 'Petrushkas' rehearsal with Wayne Sleep and Alexander Grant, London, 1975

133　'Song of a Wayfarer' with Daniel Lommel, New York, 1975

Linda Vartoogian

134   'Don Juan' with Margot Fonteyn, London, 1975

Anthony Crickmay

135   Backstage for his production of 'The Sleeping Beauty' London, 1975

Zoë Dominic

136   'Lucifer' New York, 1975

Martha Swope

137/138   'Lucifer' New York, 1975

Martha Swope

139   'Lucifer' New York, 1975

Linda Vartoogian

140   'Apollo' New York, 1974/5

Linda Vartoogian

141/142   'Apollo' New York, 1975

Linda Vartoogian

143   'Raymonda' New York, 1975

Martha Swope

144 'Raymonda' with Cynthia Gregory, New York, 1975

Linda Vartoogian

145 'Swan Lake' New York, 1975

Linda Vartoogian

146   'Swan Lake' New York, 1975

Martha Swope

147   'The Dream' London, 1976

Zoë Dominic

148   Rehearsing 'The Sleeping Beauty' Paris, 1976

149   'La Bayadère' with Monica Mason, New York, 1976

Linda Vartoogian

150   In his dressing room at the Coliseum, London, 1977

Unknown photographer

151   The Muppet Show, London, 1977

152   'Pierrot Lunaire' New York, 1977

MIRA

153   'El Penitente' New York, 1977

Linda Vartoogian

154 'Hamlet Prelude' with Margot Fonteyn, London, 1977

Leslie E. Spatt

155   Rehearsing 'The Canarsie Venus' with Murray Louis, New York, 1978

Jack Vartoogian

156   'Moment' New York, 1978

Jack Vartoogian

157   Nureyev at forty, 1978

Sally Soames

158 'The Canarsie Venus' New York, 1978

Jack Vartoogian

159   Paris, 1979

Martine Franck

160　'Le Bourgeois Gentilhomme' with Noella Pontois, Paris, 1979

161   'L'Après-midi d'un faune' with Margot Fonteyn, London, 1979

Anthony Crickmay

162   'L'Après-midi d'un faune' London, 1979

Zoë Dominic

163   'L'Après-midi d'un faune' with Charlene Gehn, New York, 1978

164   'The Idiot' with Valery Panov, Berlin, 1980

Jennie Walton

165   Rehearsing 'The Idiot' with Valery Panov, Berlin, 1980

Jennie Walton

166   Rehearsing 'Romeo and Juliet' London, 1980

Michael Ward

167   Rehearsing 'Romeo and Juliet' with Evelyn Desutter, London, 1980

Michael Ward

168　'Petrushka' Paris, 1982

Agence de Presse Bernand

169   Rehearsals for a gala TV benefit with Yehudi Menuhin, New York, 1982

Jack Vartoogian

171/172   'L'Après-midi d'un faune' Paris, 1982

Colette Masson

173　'Phaedra's Dream' Paris, 1984

Colette Masson

174   'Romeo and Juliet' Paris, 1984

Colette Masson

175   'Quelques pas graves de Baptiste' Paris, 1985

Colette Masson

176   Portrait, 1986

Snowdon

177   Return to Ufa, 1987

Unknown photographer

Biography

1938   Born on 17 March, on trans-Siberian train, near Irkutsk; son of Tartar parents.

1938–41   Lived in Moscow with family; father member of political unit of the Soviet Army.

1941   Evacuated with family to Bashkir Republic.

1943   Moved with family to Ufa.

1945–55   Studied folk dancing and music while at school in Ufa, with first ballet lessons, under Madame Udeltsova, from the age of eleven. Gained early stage experience, from the age of fifteen, doing walk-on roles for Ufa Opera House, eventually becoming apprentice member of the corps de ballet.

1955–58   Studied at the Leningrad Choreographic (Kirov) School, under Alexander Pushkin, with stage début at the Kirov Theatre, Leningrad, while a final-year student.

1958   Performed with great success at the Moscow Ballet Competition; offered contracts with both Bolshoi and the Stanislavsky and Nemirovich-Danchenko companies in Moscow. Refused both offers, returning to Leningrad and entering the Kirov Ballet as a soloist.

1958–61   Danced with the Kirov Ballet, performing leading virtuoso roles and partnering such ballerinas as Natalia Dudinskaya, Alla Shelest, Irina Kolpakova, and Alla Sizova.

1961   Appeared in Paris with the Kirov Ballet during their Paris/London tour; sought political asylum with French authorities on 17 June. Joined the Grand Ballet du Marquis de Cuevas, with first performance in a Western company in Paris on 23 June, partnering Nina Vyroubova in **The Sleeping Beauty**.

1962   Covent Garden début with Margot Fonteyn with the Royal Ballet, London, in **Giselle**.

1962–77   Principal guest artist with the Royal Ballet, forming famous partnership with Margot Fonteyn and creating roles for numerous choreographers including Frederick Ashton and Kenneth MacMillan. Also international guest artist, with appearances around the world including those for the Chicago Ballet, Stuttgart Ballet, Vienna State Opera Ballet, National Ballet of Canada, Australian Ballet, La Scala (Milan) Ballet, Dutch National Ballet, Ballet du XXe Siècle, Paul Taylor Dance Company, Royal Danish Ballet, Paris Opéra Ballet, London Festival Ballet, American Ballet Theatre, and Martha Graham Company.

1964   Staged first complete ballet, **Raymonda**, for Royal Ballet's touring company at the Spoleto Festival, Italy.

1966   Début as a choreographer with **Tancredi** for the Vienna State Opera Ballet. Staged first production of **The Sleeping Beauty** for La Scala, Milan.

1973   Received the **Dance Magazine** Award, New York, and the Prix Marius Petipa, Paris.

1974–75   Directed and danced in own season, called 'Nureyev and Friends', on Broadway, New York, leading to regular seasons in New York and London through the 1980s.

1977   Made Hollywood acting début with **Valentino**, directed by Ken Russell.

1978   Awarded the Medaille de Vermeil de la Ville de Paris.

1982   Took Austrian citizenship.

1983   Appeared in second Hollywood film, **Exposed**, directed by James Tobak.

1983–87   Artistic director of the Paris Opéra Ballet, continuing as both choreographer and principal dancer with the Paris company.

1984   Awarded the Queen Elizabeth II Coronation Award from the Royal Academy of Dancing in London.

1987   Received the title of Chevalier de la Légion d'honneur, France.

1989   Returned to Russia to appear on the Kirov stage in **La Sylphide**. Performed the leading acting and singing role of the King of Siam in the Rogers and Hammerstein musical, **The King and I**, touring the United States.

1991   Received the title of Commandeur de l'Ordre des Arts et des Lettres, France. Also made début as orchestral conductor, with performances in Vienna, Budapest and Athens.

1992   Staged final production (with Kourgapkina), the full-length **La Bayadère**, at the Paris Opéra.

1993   Died in Paris on 6 January.

Nureyev's roles

Each entry details Nureyev's first performance in a leading role in a particular ballet, the choreographer, company and location.

1957	**The Nutcracker** Vassily Vainonen / The Prince / Kirov Ballet, Leningrad	
	Swan Lake Marius Petipa and Lev Ivanov, staged by Konstantin Sergeyev / Pas de trois / Kirov Ballet, Leningrad	
1958	**Le Corsaire** (excerpt) Marius Petipa, staged by Vakhtang Chabukiani / Pas de deux / Moscow Ballet Competition, Moscow	
	Esmeralda (excerpt) Marius Petipa, staged by Vakhtang Chabukiani / 'Diana and Acteon' Pas de deux / Moscow Ballet Competition	
	Gayané (excerpts) Nina Anisimova / Kurdish Dance / Moscow Ballet Competition, Moscow	
	Laurencia Vakhtang Chabukiani / Frondoso / Kirov Ballet, Leningrad	
	The Red Poppy Rostislav Zakharov / Pas de quatre / Kirov Ballet, Leningrad	
1959–60	**Don Quixote** Alexander Gorsky after Marius Petipa / Basilio / Kirov Ballet, Leningrad	
	Giselle Marius Petipa after Jean Coralli and Jules Perrot / Albrecht / Kirov Ballet, Leningrad	
	The Sleeping Beauty Marius Petipa, staged by Konstantin Sergeyev / The Bluebird / Kirov Ballet, Leningrad	
	Raymonda Marius Petipa, staged by Konstantin Sergeyev / Kirov Ballet, Leningrad	
	Gayané Nina Anisimova / Armen / Kirov Ballet, Leningrad	
	Muskovsky Waltz Vassily Vainonen / Leading dancer / Kirov Ballet, Leningrad	
1960–61	**The Flames of Paris** (excerpt) Vassily Vainonen / Pas de deux / Kirov Ballet, Leningrad	
	Waltz Leonid Yakobson / Leading dancer / Kirov Ballet, Leningrad	created role
	Swan Lake Marius Petipa and Lev Ivanov, staged by Konstantin Sergeyev / Prince Siegfried / Kirov Ballet, Leningrad	
	The Sleeping Beauty Marius Petipa and Lev Ivanov, staged by Konstantin Sergeyev / Prince Désiré / Kirov Ballet, Leningrad	
1961	**Le Spectre de la rose** Mikhail Fokine / Title role / German television	
	The Sleeping Beauty Marius Petipa, staged by Robert Helpmann / The Bluebird / Grand Ballet du Marquis de Cuevas, Paris	
	Poème tragique Frederick Ashton / Leading role / Royal Academy of Dancing Gala	created role
1962	**La Fille mal gardée** Joseph Lazzini / Colas / Ballet de Marseille, Marseilles	
	Toccata and Fugue Erik Bruhn / Leading dancer / Nureyev–Bruhn Company, Cannes	created role
	Fantaisie Erik Bruhn / Leading dancer / Nureyev–Bruhn Company, Cannes	created role
	Dances from Raymonda Rudolf Nureyev, after Marius Petipa / Nureyev–Bruhn Company, Cannes	
	Flower Festival at Genzano (excerpts) August Bournonville, staged by Erik Bruhn / Pas de deux / Nureyev–Bruhn Company, Paris	

Les Sylphides Mikhail Fokine / Waltz and Mazurka / Royal Ballet, London

Grand Pas classique Victor Gsovsky / Leading dancer / Stuttgart Ballet Gala, Stuttgart

Prince Igor (opera by Borodin) Ruth Page and Enrique Martinez / Polovtsian Warrior / Chicago Opera and Ballet, Chicago

The Merry Widow Ruth Page / Danilo / Chicago Ballet, Chicago

Theme and Variations George Balanchine / Leading dancer / American Ballet Theatre, Chicago

1963   **Antigone** John Cranko / Etiocles / Royal Ballet, London

Diversions Kenneth MacMillan / Leading dancer / Royal Ballet, London

Marguerite and Armand Frederick Ashton / Armand / Royal Ballet, London   created role

Petrushka Mikhail Fokine / Title role / Royal Ballet, London

La Bayadère ('Kingdom of the Shades' excerpt) Marius Petipa, staged by Rudolf Nureyev / Solor / Royal Ballet, London

Fantaisie in G Minor Kenneth MacMillan / Leading dancer / Royal Academy of Dancing Gala, London   created role

Laurencia ('Pas de Six' excerpt) Vakhtang Chabukiani, staged by Rudolf Nureyev / Leading dancer / Royal Ballet, London

1964   **Images of Love** Kenneth MacMillan / Pas de trois: 'Two Loves I have' / Royal Ballet, London   created role

Hamlet Robert Helpmann / Title role / Royal Ballet, London

Divertimento Kenneth MacMillan / Leading dancer / Western Theatre Ballet Gala

Raymonda Marius Petipa, staged by Rudolf Nureyev / Jean de Brienne / Royal Ballet Touring Company, Spoleto, Italy

Swan Lake Marius Petipa and Lev Ivanov, staged by Rudolf Nureyev / Prince Siegfried / Vienna State Opera Ballet, Vienna

1965   **La Sylphide** August Bournonville, staged by Erik Bruhn / James / National Ballet of Canada, Toronto

Romeo and Juliet Kenneth MacMillan / Romeo / Royal Ballet, London   created role

1966   **Tancredi** Rudolf Nureyev / Title role / Vienna State Opera Ballet, Vienna   created role

Song of the Earth Kenneth MacMillan / The Messenger of Death / Royal Ballet, London

The Sleeping Beauty Marius Petipa, staged by Rudolf Nureyev / Prince Florimund / Ballet of La Scala, Milan

Don Quixote Marius Petipa and Alexander Gorsky, staged by Rudolf Nureyev / Basil / Vienna State Opera Ballet, Vienna

1967   **Paradise Lost** Roland Petit / The Man / Royal Ballet, London   created role

Apollo George Balanchine / Title role / Vienna State Opera Ballet, Vienna

1968   **Jazz Calendar** Frederick Ashton / Friday's Child / Royal Ballet, London   created role

A Birthday Offering Frederick Ashton / Pas de Deux and Solo / Royal Ballet, London

The Dream Frederick Ashton / Oberon / Royal Ballet Touring Company, European tour

L'Estasi Roland Petit / Man / Ballet of La Scala, Milan   created role

Monument for a Dead Boy Rudi van Dantzig / The Boy / Dutch National Ballet

1969   **Pelléas and Mélisande** Roland Petit / Pélléas / Royal Ballet, London

1970   **The Ropes of Time** Rudi van Dantzig / The Traveller / Royal Ballet, London   created role

Les Rendezvous Frederick Ashton / Variation and Adagio of Lovers / Royal Ballet, London

Apparitions (excerpt) Frederick Ashton / The Poet / Royal Ballet, London

	Dances at a Gathering Jerome Robbins / Leading dancer / Royal Ballet, London	
	Big Bertha (first version) Paul Taylor / Leading role / Paul Taylor Dance Company, New York television	created role
1971	Chant du compagnon errant Maurice Béjart / The Young Man / Ballet du XXe Siècle, Brussels	created role
	Le Sacre du printemps Maurice Béjart / The Chosen One / Ballet du XXe Siècle, Brussels	
	Field Figures Glen Tetley / Leading dancer / Royal Ballet, London	
	Checkmate Ninette de Valois / First Red Knight / Royal Ballet, London	
1972	Afternoon of a Faun Jerome Robbins / The Boy / Royal Ballet, London	
	Aureole Paul Taylor / Leading dancer / Paul Taylor Dance Company, Mexico City	
	Book of Beasts Paul Taylor / Illuminations / Paul Taylor Dance Company, Mexico City	
	Laborintus Glen Tetley / Leading dancer / Royal Ballet, London	created role
	Sideshow Kenneth MacMillan / Leading dancer / Royal Ballet, Liverpool	created role
	The Moor's Pavane José Limón / The Moor / National Ballet of Canada, American tour	
1973	Agon George Balanchine / Sarabande / Royal Ballet, London	
1974	Don Juan John Neumeier / Title role / National Ballet of Canada, tour	
	La Fille mal gardée Frederick Ashton / Colas / Royal Ballet, New York	
	Manon Kenneth MacMillan / Des Grieux / Royal Ballet, London	
	Tristan Glen Tetley / Title role / Paris Opéra Ballet, Paris	created role
1975	Coppélia Erik Bruhn after Arthur Saint-Léon, Hans Beck and Glasseman / Franz / National Ballet of Canada, London	
	Lucifer Martha Graham / Title role / Martha Graham Dance Company, New York	created role
	Sonate à trois Maurice Béjart / The Man / Scottish Ballet, Madrid	
	The Lesson Flemming Flindt / The Teacher / Scottish Ballet, Madrid	
	Moment Murray Louis / Leading dancer / Scottish Ballet, Madrid	created role
	Blown in a Gentle Wind Rudi van Dantzig / The Man / Dutch National Ballet, Amsterdam	
	Appalachian Spring Martha Graham / The Revivalist / Martha Graham Dance Company, New York	
	Night Journey Martha Graham / Oedipus / Martha Graham Dance Company, New York	
	The Scarlet Letter Martha Graham / Dimmesdale / Martha Graham Dance Company, New York	created role
1976	Four Schumann Pieces Hans van Manen / Leading dancer / National Ballet of Canada, Toronto	
1977	Pierrot Lunaire Glen Tetley / Title role / Royal Danish Ballet, Copenhagen	
	El Penitente Martha Graham / Title role / Martha Graham Dance Company, New York	
	Hamlet Prelude Frederick Ashton / Hamlet / Covent Garden Gala for Silver Jubilee of Queen Elizabeth II, London	created role
	Romeo and Juliet Kenneth MacMillan / Romeo / Royal Ballet, London	created role
	The Toreador (pas de deux) Flemming Flindt / Title role / Nureyev Festival, London	
1978	Faun Toer van Schayk / Title role / Dutch National Ballet, Amsterdam	created role
	About a Dark House Rudi van Dantzig / Leading dancer / Dutch National Ballet, Amsterdam	created role

Vivace (solo) Murray Louis / The dancer / Nureyev Festival, New York — created role

The Canarsie Venus (also The Brighton Venus) Murray Louis / The Gentleman / Murray Louis Dance Company, New York

Konservatoriet August Bournonville, staged by Mona Vangsaae / Leading role / London Festival Ballet, New York

Schéhérazade Mikhail Fokine / The Golden Slave / London Festival Ballet, New York

1979 Ulysses Rudi van Dantzig / Title role / Vienna State Opera Ballet, Vienna — created role

Le Bourgeois Gentilhomme (new version) George Balanchine, with Jerome Robbins / Cléonte / New York City Opera and Students of the School of American Ballet, New York — created role

L'Après-midi d'un faune Vaslav Nijinsky / The Faun / Joffrey Ballet, New York

1980 The Idiot Valery Panov / Prince Myshkin / German Opera Ballet, Berlin — created role

Miss Julie Birgit Cullberg / Jean, the Butler / German Opera Ballet, Berlin

Five Tangos Hans van Manen / Leading dancer / German Opera Ballet, Berlin

1981 Marco Spada Pierre Lacotte / Title role / Rome Opera Ballet, Rome — created role

1982 The Tempest Rudolf Nureyev / Prospero / Royal Ballet, London — created role

1983 Notre-Dame de Paris Roland Petit / Quasimodo / Ballet de Marseille, New York

1984 Arlequin, magicien par amour Ivo Cramér / Harlequin / Paris Opéra Ballet, Paris

Bach Suite Rudolf Nureyev and Francine Lancelot / Leading dancer / Paris Opéra Ballet, Paris

Le Sacre du printemps Glen Tetley / Leading dancer / Paris Opéra Ballet, Paris

Violin Concerto George Balanchine / Leading dancer / Paris Opéra Ballet, Paris

Romeo and Juliet Rudolf Nureyev / Mercutio / Paris Opéra Ballet, Paris

Phaedra's Dream Martha Graham / Hippolytus / Paris Opéra Ballet, Paris

1985 Quelques pas graves de Baptiste Francine Lancelot / L'Amour / Paris Opéra Ballet, Paris — created role

Washington Square Rudolf Nureyev / Dr. Sloper / Paris Opéra Ballet, Paris

The Nutcracker Rudolf Nureyev / Drosselmeyer / Paris Opéra Ballet, Paris

1986 La Dansomanie Ivo Cramér and Mary Skeaping after libretto by Pierre Gardel / M. Duléger / Paris Opéra Ballet, Paris

Manfred Rudolf Nureyev / Title role / Paris Opéra Ballet, Paris

Cendrillon Rudolf Nureyev / The Producer / Paris Opéra Ballet, Paris

1987 Two Brothers Daniel Ezralow and David Parsons / Leading dancer / Paris Opéra Ballet, Paris

1988 Orpheus George Balanchine / Title role / New York City Ballet, New York

Swan Lake Marius Petipa and Lev Ivanov, staged by Rudolf Nureyev / Von Rothbart / Paris Opéra Ballet, Paris

1989 The Overcoat Flemming Flint / Akaky Akakyevich / Maggio Musicale, Florence — created role

1990 Romeo and Juliet Kenneth MacMillan / Mercutio / Royal Ballet, London

Coppélia Dennis Nahat / Dr. Coppélius / Cleveland–San José Ballet, Edinburgh

1991 Death in Venice Flemming Flindt / Aschenbach / Verona Opera Ballet, Verona

Productions

Original choreography:

1966 **Tancredi** Hans Werner Henze / Vienna State Opera Ballet, Vienna

1977 **Romeo and Juliet** Sergei Prokofiev / London Festival Ballet, London (also 1980: La Scala, Milan / 1984: Paris Opéra Ballet)

1979 **Manfred** Peter Ilyich Tchaikovsky / Paris Opéra Ballet, Paris (also 1981: Zurich Ballet)

1982 **The Tempest** Peter Ilyich Tchaikovsky / Royal Ballet, London (also 1984: Paris Opéra Ballet)

1984 **Bach Suite** (with Lancelot) Johann Sebastian Bach / Paris Opéra Ballet, Paris

1985 **Washington Square** Charles Ives / Paris Opéra Ballet, Paris

1986 **Cendrillon** Sergei Prokofiev / Paris Opéra Ballet, Paris

Restagings of classics:

1962 **Le Corsaire** (Pas de deux, after Marius Petipa) Riccardo Drigo, Léon Minkus / Bell Telephone television programme, New York

Gayané (Pas de deux, after Nina Anisimova) Aram Khachaturian / American Ballet Theatre, New York

1963 **La Bayadère** ('Kingdom of the Shades' scene, after Marius Petipa, Vakhtang Chabukiani) Léon Minkus / Royal Ballet, London (also 1974: Paris Opéra Ballet)

The Flames of Paris (Pas de deux, after Vassily Vainonen) Boris Asafiev / Royal Academy of Dancing Gala, London

1964 **Raymonda** (after Marius Petipa) Alexander Glazunov / Royal Ballet Touring Company, Spoleto (also 1965: Australian Ballet / 1972: Zurich Ballet / 1975: American Ballet Theatre / 1983: Paris Opéra Ballet)

Swan Lake (after Marius Petipa, Lev Ivanov) Peter Ilyich Tchaikovsky / Vienna State Opera Ballet, Vienna (also 1984: Paris Opéra Ballet / 1990: La Scala, Milan)

Paquita Grand Pas (after Marius Petipa) Léon Minkus / Royal Academy of Dancing Gala, London (also 1971: Vienna State Opera Ballet)

1965 **Laurencia Pas de Six** (after Vakhtang Chabukiani) Alexander Krien / Royal Ballet, London

1966 **The Sleeping Beauty** (after Marius Petipa) Peter Ilyich Tchaikovsky / Ballet of La Scala, Milan (also 1972: National Ballet of Canada / 1975: London Festival Ballet / 1980: Vienna State Opera Ballet / 1992: German Opera Ballet, Berlin)

Don Quixote (after Marius Petipa) Léon Minkus, arranged by John Lanchbery / Vienna State Opera Ballet, Vienna (also 1970: Australian Ballet / 1979: Zurich Ballet / 1981: Paris Opéra Ballet / 1985: Peking Opera Ballet, Matsuyama Ballet)

1967 **The Nutcracker** (after Lev Ivanov, Vassily Vainonen) Peter Ilyich Tchaikovsky / Royal Swedish Ballet, Stockholm (also 1968: Royal Ballet / 1971: Teatro Colón, Buenos Aires / 1971: La Scala, Milan / 1979: German Opera Ballet, Berlin / 1985: Paris Opéra Ballet)

1992 **La Bayadère** (with Kourgapkina, after Marius Petipa) Léon Minkus / Paris Opéra Ballet, Paris

Film, television and videos

1962   The Bell Telephone Hour, New York television

1963   An Evening with the Royal Ballet, including Laurencia (after Chabukiani), 'Golden Hour' British television

1966   Romeo and Juliet (MacMillan) with Margot Fonteyn
Le Jeune Homme et la mort (Petit), with Zizi Jeanmaire
Burt Bacharach Special, performing Paul Taylor's Big Bertha, New York television (CBS)
Swan Lake (own staging), with the Vienna State Opera Ballet

1972   The Sleeping Beauty (own staging), with National Ballet of Canada, Canadian television (CBC)
Don Quixote (own staging and direction), with Australian Ballet
I am a Dancer, documentary

1977   Valentino, Hollywood film directed by Ken Russell

1978   Video Sera (dir. Vittoria Ottolenghi), Italian televion (RAI 1)

1980   Tim, Tam (dir. Vittoria Ottolenghi), Italian television (RAI 1)
Julie Andrews' Invitation to the Dance
Giselle, with Carla Fracci, Rome Opera

1982   Romeo and Juliet (Nureyev version) at La Scala, Milan
Dedicated to Diaghilev, British television (BBC)

1983   Exposed, Hollywood film directed by James Tobak
Raymonda (own staging), with the Paris Opéra Ballet, French television (Antenne 2)
L'Autre (dir. Paolo Calvetti), Italian television (RAI 2)

1984   Nureyev – Dupond (dir. Paolo Calvetti), Italian television (RAI 2)
The Tempest (Nureyev), and Arlequin, magicien par amour (Cramér), French television (Antenne 2)

1986   Initiation of the Five: Washington Square (Nureyev)

1987   Cendrillon (Nureyev) with the Paris Opéra Ballet

1988   The Nutcracker (Nureyev) with the Paris Opéra Ballet

1989   Coup de foudre, television film with Michel Legrand

1992   Nureyev (dir. Patricia Foy), Antelope Films, London

1993   Noureev, mémoire d' une Bayadère (dir. Catherine Dupuis), extracts of La Bayadère with Paris Opéra Ballet

Publications

Barnes, Clive, Nureyev, New York, 1982
Bland, Alexander, The Nureyev Image, London and New York, 1976
Bland, Alexander, Fonteyn and Nureyev: The Story of a Partnership, London, 1979
Bland, Alexander, The Royal Ballet: The First Fifty Years, London, 1981
Cruikshank, Judith, 'Nureyev Looks Forward' (interview), Dance and Dancers (London), June 1982
Deletraz, François, 'Ce qu'ils pensent de lui', Les Saisons de la danse (Paris), November 1981
Dupuis, Simone, 'Noureev, 20 ans en France', Les Saisons de la danse (Paris), November 1981
Fonteyn, Margot, Margot Fonteyn: An Autobiography, London, 1975
Geitel, K., Der Tanzer Rudolf Nurejew, 1967
Gruen, John, 'The Force Still with Us', Dance Magazine (New York), July 1986
Kersley, Leo, and Sinclair, Janet, 'Nureyev', Ballet Today (London), June 1962
Money, Keith, The Art of the Royal Ballet, London, 1964
Nureyev, Rudolf, Nureyev: An Autobiography with Pictures, edited by Alexander Bland, London, 1962; New York, 1964
Percival, John, Nureyev, New York, 1975; London, 1976
'Rudolf Noureev' (various authors), Special issue, L'Avant-scène: Ballet/Danse (Paris), 1983
Saal, H., 'Tartar of the Dance', Newsweek (New York), 19 April 1965
Sklarevskaya, I., 'Nureyev at the Kirov', translated by R. Johnson, Dance Magazine (New York), May 1990
Smakov, Gennady, The Great Russian Dancers, New York, 1984
Vollmer, Jurgen (photographs) and Devere, John (text), Nureyev in Paris: Le Jeune Homme et la mort, New York, 1975

Photographic acknowledgements:
Andes Press Agency: 170
Associated Press: 89
Camera Press, London/Snowdon: 176
Collection Jennie Walton: 5
Hulton-Deutsch Collection: 13, 102, 105, 132, 150, 151, 160
Magnum Photos Ltd, London: 16–17, 46–48, 54–55, 159
MIRA/Myra Armstrong: 123, 124
Rex Features Ltd, London: 1–4, 6–9, 24–25, 73–77, 80, 93, 106, 117, 126, 148, 177
Sotheby's, London: 57–58
Photographs by Anthony Crickmay and Houston Rogers are from the collections of the Theatre Museum, reproduced by courtesy of the Trustees of the Victoria and Albert Museum, London.